# Stirling Castle

**HISTORIC** **SCOTLAND**

Historic Buildings and Monuments

Text by Richard Fawcett

Designed by
HMSO Graphic Design
Edinburgh

Principal photography by
Sean Hudson

Subsidiary photography by
John Reiach

ISBN 0 11 491992 5

Edinburgh
Her Majesty's Stationery Office

*Grateful thanks for permission to
reproduce photographs to*

The Scottish Tourist Board
The Royal Commission on the
Ancient and Historical Monu-
ments of Scotland
The National Library of Scotland
The Scottish National Portrait
Gallery
The Scottish Record Office

The Royal Abbey of Augustinian Canons at Cambuskenneth.

# A Short History

Stirling and Edinburgh are perhaps the two castles which are most closely identified with the secular history of Scotland. Those who have visited them will recognise a number of features in common, both in the nature of their sites, and in the way that the various structures have been laid out. Each castle occupies a secure volcanic outcrop, which has been made even more easily defensible by the scraping of glaciers in the Ice Ages. (This same action has in each case left a gentle tail-like ridge at one end of the outcrop, along which a dependant town could develop.) In addition both castles were favoured residences of successive Scottish Kings, who progressively rebuilt in the prevailing taste of their times to meet expanding needs, and in a number of cases rebuilding of particular features must have taken place simultaneously within the two.

For much of the middle ages the effective capital of the kingdom was wherever the King happened to be in residence, and as a result the town of Stirling, like Edinburgh, shows many of the characteristics of a medieval capital. Both were provided with fine parish churches, which eventually achieved collegiate status. Both also had a magnificent royal abbey of Augustinian canons founded in the vicinity by David I: Cambuskenneth at Stirling, and Holyrood at Edinburgh. A further likeness between the two may be seen in the surviving portions of aristocratic town houses which gathered like moths around the light sources of the royal residences, of which the Argyll Lodging and Mar's Wark at Stirling are the best remaining examples.

The Argyll Lodging, Stirling, town house of the Earls (later Dukes) of Argyll.

The positioning of a royal castle was not, of course, a matter of random choice, and at Stirling the decision to fortify the rock was dictated by the supreme strategic importance of the area. Set at the highest navigable point of the Forth, and on the line of the main pass through the hills from the north, it guarded both the principal north-south and east-west routes across Scotland. The coincidence of strategic significance and naturally strong site could hardly have been a happier one

The town of Stirling and the Military Prison from the Forework.

for the rulers of Scotland, and it is tempting to assume that the Castle rock must have been fortified for a very long period. The evidence for prehistoric forts on a number of the surrounding hills may be thought to support this assumption, as may the likely identification of Stirling with the city of Iudeu, which figures in accounts of British kings in the seventh century. However, Stirling Castle does not begin to appear in recorded history until the early 12th century, by which time it already seems to have been a residence of the Canmore dynasty of Kings.

Alexander I is the first King to be firmly identified with the Castle: he founded a chapel here, and it was probably within the walls of the Castle that he died in 1124. The Castle next comes on record exactly fifty years later, when it was handed over to Henry II of England, along with five other castles, to pay for William the Lion's release after his capture at the Battle of Alnwick. Scottish control of the Castle was regained in 1189, and twenty-five years after that date King William died within it. In all this time we have no idea of its physical appearance, although we may guess that many of the buildings would have been of timber. The Castle probably began to assume a more permanent masonry form only in the late 13th century, and we have references to new masonwork in 1287; but the turmoil of the succeeding century was to obliterate all recognizable traces of this work.

As one of the most important castles in the Kingdom, Stirling naturally played a major part in the Scottish struggle for independence of English overlordship. In 1291 Edward I took custody of all Scottish royal castles whilst he adjudicated on who was the rightful King of Scotland, and the Castle's history over the next fifty years is mainly that of a struggle for its occupation by the forces fighting on behalf of the rival claimants. During the course of this struggle Stirling was the scene of several of the finest triumphs of the Scottish patriots –although the benefits derived from these triumphs were often short-lived enough. In 1297 the army of William Wallace and Andrew Moray, which was gathered on

The medieval bridge at Stirling was placed at a strategically important crossing of the Forth.

Abbey Craig to the north-east of the Castle, overthrew the English in a famous victory at Stirling Bridge, and thus secured the Castle for a time. However, Moray was killed in this battle and the Castle was again in English hands by the following year.

One of the most notable sieges of the Castle took place in 1304, by which time Stirling was the only castle left to the patriots. In that year Edward I instigated a successful attack, using fire-throwing equipment and a siege machine known ominously as the "War Wolf". But the victories won by the first Edward were not followed up by his son, Edward II, and by 1313 the situation was again reversed, with Stirling as one of only three castles still held by the English. It was the English attempt to relieve their garrison here which resulted in the Scottish victory at Bannockburn on Midsummer's day of the next year. Following this victory Robert I (the Bruce) ordered that the Castle should be rendered indefensible, so that it could not be held against him again. However, in the disturbances which followed his death it was once again repaired and occupied by English forces, until they were constrained to surrender to Robert the Steward (later to be Robert II) in 1342.

From the later 14th century onwards there is written evidence of a great deal of building activity, and a reference to a North Gate in 1381 may refer to the nucleus of that structure in its present form, which therefore appears to be the earliest identifiable building in the Castle

The Bannockburn monument to Robert the Bruce.

still to survive. In the course of the 14th and 15th centuries Stirling continued to provide a prominent backdrop to the continuous turbulence of medieval Scotland. Amongst the best-remembered of such events was the murder by James II within the Castle of William, eighth Earl of Douglas, in 1452, followed by the ejection of his mutilated corpse from a window.

The esteem in which the Castle was held as a Royal residence continued to increase throughout the 15th century, and probably reached its climax in the first half of the 16th century during the reigns of James IV and V, both of whom were prodigious builders. It was the former who erected the great defensive Forework across the main approach to the Castle in about 1500, and who was probably also chiefly responsible for forming the splendid royal courtyard now known as the Upper Square in the same years. Although the Great Hall is the only one of the buildings around the Square to survive in a form which would be recognised by James IV, there are reasons to think he may also have had a hand in the predecessors of the other three buildings which now flank the Square. However, it was James V who around 1540 built the most imposing of these buildings, the Palace, on the south side of the Square; its classical forms must have seemed astoundingly cosmopolitan when it was built, and they may have been the result of an influx of French masons following the King's two successive marriages to French Princesses.

Further events which have earned the Castle a place in Scottish folk memory took place in the reign of Mary Queen of Scots; amongst these were her coronation within the Chapel in 1543, her escape from death by fire in 1561, and the baptism of her son, the future James VI, in 1566. It is less well-known that her reign was also of some architectural significance for the Castle. In 1559 her mother, Mary of Guise, who was Regent during the Queen's residence in France, installed a French garrison in the Castle in the course of her struggle with the Reformers. Traditionally at the same time she is said to have been responsible for a spur-shaped battery and its associated works, which were constructed in front of James IV's Forework and which survived until the early 18th century. There are good reasons for accepting the tradition which makes Mary responsible for the Spur, and for seeing it as the counterpart of a similar feature at Edinburgh Castle, which had been built by an Italian engineer in the previous decade. Recent investigation has suggested that part of the spur at Stirling still survives, embodied in the later defences.

James VI, who as a baby had been crowned in the parish church at Stirling, had a close connection with the Castle throughout his occasionally precarious Scottish reign. The struggles between the various factions to dominate the youthful King were at times centred on the Castle, and with such memories it may be thought surprising that James chose to spend so much time at Stirling later; perhaps it was its security which attracted him. In 1594 his first son, Prince Henry, was born here, and remodelling of the Chapel was immediately begun to provide an appropriate setting for his baptism. There were also grandiose schemes for reconstruction of other buildings, many of which appear to have been in a poor state of repair by this time. Most of these ideas were abandoned, however, when in 1603 James moved south to accept the English Crown, and despite a promise of regular "homecomings" the Castle now entered a twilight phase of royal occupation.

Nevertheless, over the following decades considerable works were under-

Reconstruction drawing of the Great Hall as it might have been in the early 16th century. (RCAHMS.)

taken to keep the buildings in some sort of repair, most notably in anticipation of a royal visit in 1617. Further repairs were made on the accession of Charles I in 1625, and again before his visit to Scotland in 1633, although these works have a half-hearted air to them: despite the fact that England and Scotland were still two separate kingdoms, the very limited need for royal residences in the northern kingdom hardly justified the cost of their upkeep. The next royal visit was by Charles II in 1650, the year after his father's execution, when he attempted to consolidate his Scottish support; but by the following year the Castle was in the hands of Parliamentary forces, as a consequence of a briskly conducted siege under the command of General Monk.

A number of repairs and alterations followed the Restoration of the monarchy in 1660, although these were insufficient to prevent the Castle being "mightily out of repair" by the early 18th century. We are fortunate that from the later 17th century onwards there exists a series of detailed plans and other drawings, since they help us to visualise the various modifications which were made to the Castle over the ensuing centuries, even if what they chiefly illustrate is the conversion of a royal Castle and Palace into a fortress and barrack. The Revolution which ousted James VII in 1689, and led to an immediate strengthening of the defences of Stirling, was to create severely divided loyalties in Scotland, which were not mollified by the Union of the Kingdom in 1707. Threat of French-supported rebellion as a result of the Act of Union led to the major reconstruction of the Outer Defences to the form which we now see. In 1708 Captain Theodore Dury, Engineer in North Britain, started construction of the new defences, and despite their having to be drastically remodelled in the course of construction following complaints on their inadequacy, they seem to have been completed by 1714.

Whilst this work was in progress proposals were also made for remodelling the principal buildings around the Upper Square for royal residence perhaps to

James VI by Bronckorst and Mary Queen of Scots by an unknown artist.

John, Earl of Mar (1675-1732) by Kneller.

The exiled Earl of Mar's proposals for remodelling the Palace.

assure Scotland of continued royal interest–although they were never put into effect. An extraordinary series of further designs for the Palace block was drawn up in 1724 by the exiled Jacobite, John, Earl of Mar (1675-1732), whose predecessors (and successors after 1923) were hereditary Keepers of the Castle. This Earl, who had led the Scottish forces that rose in support of the Old Pretender in 1715, was a man of considerable architectural skills, and his designs for a remodelled Palace to house the restored Stewart dynasty show great imagination. However, the last possibility of making Stirling the setting of a brilliant court for James VII's descendants passed with the Young Pretender's abortive attempt to take the Castle in 1746.

The spacious royal planning of 15th and 16th century Stirling Castle was no longer suitable for an army barrack, and throughout the 18th century the buildings were gradually sub-divided and adapted to their altered circumstances. The last building operation of any significance to take place followed a fire at the northern end of the King's Old Building in 1855. Although the subsequent reconstruction to the designs of Robert Billings has not been universally admired, it should be understood as a conscientious attempt to create a building with historically-inspired detailing which would be worthy of its setting. Perhaps more significantly, it may be seen as an indicator of a growing awareness of the value of a group of buildings whose exalted origins had been all but obliterated beneath an unworthy veneer of later adaptations.

As the 19th century continued there was a growing current of feeling that some attempt should be made to rescue at least the finest of the buildings, although the continued military use of the Castle was a major obstacle to this. A preliminary step was taken in 1906, following the personal intervention of Edward VII, when the maintenance of the Castle was transferred to the Office of Works. Under the new arrangements there was to be a more historically-directed approach to the buildings, and a policy of revealing features of interest wherever possible. Two results of this were the exposure of the 16th century kitchens below the Grand Battery, and the removal of sub-divisions within the Chapel Royal.

But it was not until the Castle ceased to function as a Regimental Depot in 1964 that it became feasible to consider systematic treatment of the Castle as a group of structures of the highest historic and architectural value. The work which this has entailed has been in progress since then, and will continue for several years yet, since the greatest care has to be taken to evaluate all of the evidence embodied within the buildings themselves. It is hoped that visitors will understand that this work inevitably makes it necessary to limit access, or to close parts of the Castle periodically.

*Bottom right* Prince Charles Edward, the Young Pretender, by David.

The Castle in the late 17th century, John Slezer's *Theatrum Scotiae*.

# A Tour of the Castle

Stirling Castle is a complex group of buildings, which is well worth an extended visit. However, for the benefit of those visitors with limited time this tour has been divided into two consecutive sections: the first part (nos 1-8) includes the most important buildings of the Castle, which should be seen by everyone; the second part (nos 9-16), which extends the tour to include the other parts open to the public, could be omitted by visitors who are short of time.

The volcanic rock on which the Castle stands is aligned from the north-west to the south-east. The natural approach to it is from the south-east, where the action of glaciers left a long and gradually sloping tail along which the medieval town developed, and it was along this side that the chief defences were concentrated. At the head of the tail, and in front of the Castle, an open area, now known as the Esplanade, was left so that enemies could not approach too closely without exposing themselves to the fire of defenders. In about 1809 this area was flattened to serve as a parade-ground, which now provides an excellent visual foil to the Outer Defences of the Castle.

In the 16th century, probably in 1559, a great spur-shaped artillery battery had been built out towards the Esplanade, with a smaller flanking battery, later known as the French Spur, to the right of it. These were to condition the design of the present Outer Defences, which were built between 1708 and 1714 at a time when the Government feared a rising in favour of the deposed line of James VII. As first designed the new defences were to have taken the form of a vast outer enclosure, planned with little regard for the theories of artillery fortification, and the beginning of the southern wall of this enclosure may still be seen projecting from the left-

hand end of the Castle's outer face. However, the engineer, Theodore Dury, was eventually constrained to adopt a more compact and effective design. The east wall of the Spur was retained, and extended to the full width of the rock, with a continuation of the ditch along the extension. The flanking French Spur was also retained (with some changes) to provide defensive fire along the outer face of the wall, and in addition caponiers (firing galleries–one of which has been destroyed) were placed in the ditch. A drawbridge crossed the ditch and opened into an enclosed area, now known as the Guardroom Square. Within this first enclosure any attackers who had penetrated so far would be at the mercy of surrounding fire. (The area is now partly occupied by 19th century structures, including a Guardroom from which the Square derives its name, a stable and a straw store.) The approach to the Inner Gate, through a wall at right angles to the outer wall, was defended by a second ditch and bridge. On the other side of this ditch a transe passes through the massive thickness of the defences, a thickness which is partly due to ranges of vaulted barrack rooms being built up against the walls for extra strength.

*Above* the surviving caponier in the outer ditch and *Left* the door into the missing caponier.

*Right* Guardroom Square and the Inner Ditch.

9

## 2. THE FOREWORK

Within the Outer Defences is the open area called the Counterguard, which is crossed at its narrowest point by a ramp leading to the gate at the centre of the cross defence known as the Forework. The Forework was built by James IV around the first decade of the 16th century, possibly incorporating parts of an earlier cross wall. It extends across the full width of the Castle rock, and was punctuated by a rectangular tower at each end, a central gatehouse with drum-towers at its outer corners (in front of which there used to be a ditch), and a pair of semi-circular towers placed symmetrically to either side of the gate. The part of this work which has survived most completely is the Prince's Tower, at the western (left-hand) end, but several of the other parts have been either extensively altered or destroyed. The Elphinstone tower, at the other end of the Forework from the Prince's tower, was reduced in the 17th century (perhaps in 1689) to provide a platform for an artillery battery, whilst the intermediate semi-circular towers have been almost completely destroyed. The principal focus of the Forework was intended to be the gate, as may now be best appreciated in late 17th century engravings, but it was cut down in the 18th century, and the present crenellations which crown it were added in the following century. Even in its present partly-mutilated state the Forework is most impressive, and must have formed a splendid frontispiece to a royal residence when it was the first part of the Castle to be seen on approaching from the town. However, it may be doubted if it would have provided any great resistance to the artillery which was developing into an effective threat to fortifications at that time, and it is not surprising that it was so soon thought expedient to provide an outer defensive skin on this most vulnerable side of the Castle.

A loop-hole in the Forework.

A Forework gateway.

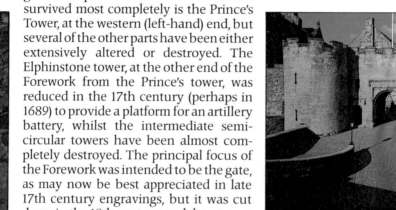

The Forework built by James IV.

The Forework Gate and *Right* the Main Guard House and Fort Major's House.

The Great Hall in use as a barrack.

## 3. THE LOWER SQUARE

Inside the Forework is the Lower Square, which is partly flanked by buildings dating from the royal occupation of the Castle, and partly by structures erected during its life as a barrack. To the left of the Square is the magnificent east front of the Palace, and directly ahead is the south gable of the Great Hall, both of which may be numbered amongst the finest buildings of their type in Europe. To the right are two much smaller buildings of late 18th or early 19th century date. The further of the two was built as the Main Guard House of the Castle, and is a handsome structure in the best traditions of military architecture, with an open arcaded loggia at the centre of its ground floor. The nearer building, which is of more recent date, has served amongst other uses as a residence for the Fort Major.

The road to the Upper Square.

The Palace.

## 4. THE UPPER SQUARE

The Upper Square is reached by a road passing between the Palace and Great Hall, and is at the heart of the Castle (it may be compared with Crown Square in Edinburgh Castle). It is entirely enclosed by the four most important buildings of the royal residence, and, even after three centuries of military use, it still provides one of the clearest evocations of the archi-tectural setting of Scottish monarchy at the end of the middle ages and the beginning of the modern period. The buildings which now extend around the sides of the Square are of a variety of dates, but it was possibly James IV who first conceived and laid out this great formal courtyard to a regular plan.

*Top to bottom*
The Chapel Royal.
The King's Old Building.
The Palace.
The Great Hall.

James IV.

The Great Hall in use as a barrack.

13

*Top right* a painted representation of a window.

The earliest reference which we have to the Castle, in 1124, is to a chapel and so we may be sure the Castle contained at least one such building throughout the middle ages–although we cannot be certain of its precise situation until the very end of that period. The importance of the ecclesiastical establishment of the Chapel Royal was to be enormously increased by James IV, who in 1501 obtained the Pope's approval to establish a college of priests, and lavishly endowed it by diverting money from other ecclesiastical sources. Shortly afterwards the Bishop of Whithorn was made Dean of the College, a clear sign of its great importance. It is likely that such a major reorganisation was either preceded or accompanied by the rebuilding of the Chapel, and it is possible that foundations found on the northern side of the square, below the later Chapel (marked out on the surface of the courtyard) are of this Chapel. These foundations are parallel to the north curtain wall of the upper part of the Castle, and further parallel foundations have been found below the entrance of the Palace, suggesting that the upper square was of rhomboidal plan in the later middle ages.

Although the present form of the Chapel Royal is a result of reconstruction by James VI in 1594, following the birth of his son, Prince Henry, there are some reasons for believing it may incorporate an earlier building. It is a handsome rectangular building with three pairs of windows within arched frames, to either side of a central doorway designed in the form of a classical triumphal arch. In 1628 the ceiling and upper walls were decorated with paintings by Valentine Jenkin, but before that date its interior was probably rather plain. In 1709/10 there were proposals to provide a new Chapel in a sub-division of the Great Hall, and to insert floors and staircases in the existing building; although this was not then done it was prophetic of what was to happen to the building later. By 1911, when the Scottish Ecclesiological Society began to agitate for the restoration of the Chapel Royal, it contained a school and dining hall at a lower level, with stores on an inserted upper floor. Eventually, in the 1930s the inserted floors and ceilings were removed, revealing the surviving fragments of the 1628 paintings.

The door of the Chapel Royal.

Valentine Jenkin's painted decoration in the Chapel.

## 6. THE KING'S OLD BUILDING

The King's Old Building, on the west side of the square is still only partly understood. Externally it now appears to be largely of 18th and 19th century date, but internal alterations have recently revealed traces of what may be the earliest surviving royal apartment in the Castle. Fragments of doors and windows suggest that by the early 16th century the main body of the range consisted of two spacious rooms lit by handsome windows, which were raised above a vaulted basement, and reached by a wide spiral stair at their southern end. The possible incorporation of earlier structures at each end, along with many later adaptations, have made it difficult to determine how much additional accommodation the building contained. But the principal rooms were clearly very fine, and almost certainly intended for royal use, suggesting it may be the 'King's House' known to have been under construction in 1496.

By the early 18th century the building was simply described as 'Officers' Lodgings', althought by 1719, when more information becomes available, it housed various functions. At one end were apartments for the Major and Chaplain, and at another was an Infirmary, whilst the main body was simply used for storage and other mundane functions. Following a fire in 1855 the architect Robert Billings recased the northern end of the range, added a projecting stair, and made considerable alterations throughout. The room on which he lavished greatest attention was that in which it used to be thought that James II murdered the Earl of Douglas. In recent years the building has again been adapted, to provide for the Regimental Museum and Headquarters of the Argyll and Sutherland Highlanders.

*Left* the Regimental Museum of the Argyll and Sutherland Regiment.

The arms of Douglas in the Douglas Room window.

The Douglas Room.

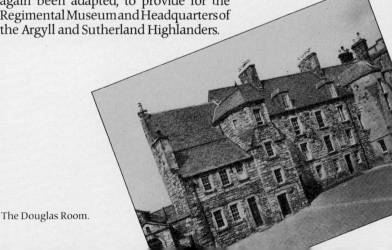

13

7

4

15

2

1

3

11

16

Francisco Ramos

# KEY

1 The Outer Defences
2 The Forework
3 The Lower Square
4 The Upper Square
5 The Chapel Royal
6 The King's Old Building
7 The Palace
8 The Great Hall

9 The North Gate and Nether Bailey
10 The Kitchens
11 The Elphinstone Tower
12 The Wall Walk
13 The 'Lady's Hole' and 'King's Knot'
14 The 'Lion's Den' and Counterguard
15 The Outer Defences
16 The French Spur

Close examination of the lower storey of the Palace, and foundations discovered in the course of excavations, indicate that there were earlier buildings on its site; some of these were probably contemporary with James IV's forework, against which the Palace was built. The existing building was under construction for James V in the 1540s and is of outstanding historical and architectural importance, both for its external appearance and for its planning. Externally the attempt to create classical facades was amongst the earliest of such attempts in Britain, and this was almost certainly a result of the influence of French masons imported by James V. The external prominence given to the principal rooms on the first floor, by means of alternating windows and shallow cusped-headed niches containing statues on balusters, shows an awareness of French royal buildings, despite the elements introduced into the design by Scottish craftsmen. The ranks of statues, which include the Devil, a selection of the Planetary Gods, and a representation of James V himself, repay close inspection.

Internally the principal floor is divided into apartments for the King and Queen, which are ranged around three sides of a central courtyard known as the "Lions' Den". (There were further rooms on the west side, but we do not know their use, since this part of the Palace collapsed in the 17th century.) The entrance to the Palace was through a porch at the north-west corner, where a door on the left opened into the first of the three main

Sculpture on the south face of Palace.

James V's initials above a window.

The angel string course.

rooms of the King's apartment. The sequence of these rooms was the King's Outer Hall, Own Hall and Bed Chamber (known by the early 18th century as the Guardhall, Presence Chamber and Bed Chamber, respectively). The King also had smaller and more intimate closets leading off his Bed Chamber, one of which probably served as a study or office. A similar apartment for the Queen was reached along a western gallery, with the Bed Chambers of the two apartments adjoining each other. The fine fireplaces show that the main rooms must have been very imposing, and a further clue to their internal decoration is provided by the splendid carved heads from the ceilings of the King's apartment, which are now displayed on the walls of the two Halls of the Queen's apartment. These heads were removed from the ceilings in 1777, after several had already fallen, and the surviving examples (except for three in the National Museum) were only finally restored to the Castle in 1970.

By the time of a survey made in 1719 the principal and lower floors of the Palace were used for little more than storage, although the present porch and stair had already been built at the north-west corner to provide access to what had become the Governor's apartment on the upper floor. The main rooms on the principal floor were subsequently adapted to barrack accommodation.

Three of the Stirling Heads.

The Queen's outer hall.

Passage below the Palace.

Entrance to the Palace.

James III.

The Great Hall is reached from the Palace by a neo-Gothic bridge across the road between the Lower and Upper Squares. In its present form this charming feature is relatively modern, although it perpetuates a means of access which seems to have been created at the time of the construction of the Palace, in order to provide communication from the royal apartments to the dais end of the hall. There would have been a Great Hall in the Castle throughout the middle ages to serve the purpose of a principal communal room, but it is not known whether its predecessors occupied the site of the present structure. The Hall which we now see is traditionally attributed to James III, although it is almost certainly mainly the work of James IV, during whose reign there are references to its construction around 1500. By the time it was built the provision of a greater range of accommodation elsewhere in the Castle would have meant that the functions of a Great Hall were no longer the same as they had been earlier in the middle ages. At Stirling, as at Edinburgh, the Hall was clearly intended primarily as a setting for major ceremonial and state occasions, rather than for daily mundane usage.

As a consequence of the steep slope of the site it was necessary to create a level platform for the Hall by constructing a vaulted basement. As was usual the Hall was a basically rectangular room and its principal entrance was towards the north end of the west wall, where there would have been a timber-screened vestibule to reduce draughts and provide a serving area. The separate royal entrance which was created at the time of the erection of the Palace has already been mentioned. Two spiral staircases at the north end gave access to a musicians' loft above the screened vestibule at the entrance, and to the walkway around the wallhead, whilst a third stair led to a balcony near the middle of the east wall, which overlooked the main body of the hall. There was also a fourth stair leading down to the basement, although this appears to have been blocked by the early 18th century, if not before. This vast space was heated by five large fireplaces, and covered by a magnificent hammer-beam ceiling. The main source of natural lighting was a series of paired windows placed high enough in the walls to allow hangings to be suspended along the lower walls; there were also two large projecting bay windows to either side of the royal dais, which rose from floor to ceiling and emphasised the prominence of the high table. In its completed state the Great Hall was in the very grandest tradition of royal halls, although as such it was still essentially a medieval concept: the dawning of a new age must have been made abundantly apparent when the Palace rose adjacent to it.

By the early 18th century such a vast hall was a white elephant in a royal palace, and in 1709/10 it was suggested that it should be cut into two parts to create a smaller banqueting hall and adjacent chapel. No action seems to have followed this suggestion, although by 1719 it had been partly broken up by the introduction of a floor above part of its length; it was only around the turn of the 18th and 19th centuries that its character was almost completely masked when it was subdivided into a series of barrack rooms by the insertion of floors and cross walls. Proposals to restore it as a Hall were made in 1893, and again in 1946, but it was not until the army left in 1964 that it became possible to seriously investigate undertaking such an operation. Since then the cross-walls and floors have been removed, and the work of restoration is proceeding slowly enough to allow full assessment of all the evidence for the original design which has been found to have survived the barrack conversion.

In use as a barrack.

In course of restoration.

At this point visitors with insufficient time for an extended visit may choose to leave the Castle; those who wish to explore the rest of the Castle should walk down the road leading to the North Gate.

## 9. THE NORTH GATE AND NETHER BAILEY

After the erection of the Great Hall the area to its east was for many years enclosed as a service court for the Hall, and contained the "King's Office Houses". However, the area was also crossed by the road leading down into the lower enclosure of the Castle, the Nether Bailey, and this road had earlier been a principal secondary route through the Castle. It originally entered the Castle through a postern (back gate) in the Nether Bailey, from where it passed through the North Gate and along the east side of the Hall to reach the Lower Square. The postern gate may have been blocked, in order to remove a potentially weak point in the Castle's circuit of walls, as early as the later 17th century, and after that the road simply served as a connection between the upper part of the Castle and the Nether Bailey. The North Gate, through which the road passed, has been greatly altered at a variety of periods, but it may incorporate the earliest surviving building in the Castle, since there is a record of work on a gate here in 1381. Traditionally the upper part of the gate was known as the Mint, but there is no evidence that the Royal Mint was ever in fact housed here—or, indeed, within the Castle. We know little of the early history of the Gate's superstructure but it was apparently remodelled in the 16th century to contain a kitchen for the Great Hall. This kitchen seems to have communicated with a service gallery which was constructed against the north wall of the Hall at about the same time, although the building which connected the two has been no more than a ruined shell since at least the later 17th century.

Visitors who wish to do so are able to descend through the North Gate into the Nether Bailey, and a walk around its walls provides excellent views across the surrounding countryside. The only buildings within this area are of the 19th century and later. The structure closest to the gate was built to house punishment cells, but was later converted into a store; the very long building within enclosed walls to the north-west of that was first built as three separate magazines, but in 1908 they were connected together and converted into mobilisation stores; the two smaller buildings in the adjoining enclosure beyond were annexes to the magazines. All were designed in the most functional manner, but are nevertheless interesting examples of their class of military structure.

The curtain wall of the Nether Bailey.

The Nether Bailey.

Excavation of the
Kitchens in 1921.

Returning through the North Gate visitors will find a descending flight of steps in front of the house beyond and to the left of the Gate (this house has served as Master Gunner's and Barrack Warden's Quarters amongst other uses). The steps lead down into a cavernous sequence of vaulted kitchens and other offices, which perhaps superseded the kitchens above the North Gate in the course of the 16th century; there is a recorded construction of kitchens in 1542 which could refer to this range . But in 1689, at the time of the troubles of the Revolution, and by which time they were probably redundant, it was decided they had to be sacrificed to the defensive needs of the Castle. Consequently their vaults were removed and they were infilled to provide a solid platform for an artillery battery. It was only in 1921 that they were re-opened for most of their length, and their vaults reconstructed.

## 11. THE ELPHINSTONE TOWER

On leaving the kitchens visitors should return to the Lower Square, passing one of the Castle's wells *en route*. In the eastern corner of the Square, behind the Main Guard House is what survives of the Elphinstone Tower, the rectangular tower at the eastern end of James IV's Forework. Originally this tower would have been as tall as its counterpart at the other end of the Forework, the Prince's Tower, but it was cut down to provide a platform for a 3-gun battery–perhaps at the same time that the 16th century kitchens were infilled. The protective parapet, or breastwork, was later re-modelled again by Theodore Dury, when he was reconstructing the Outer Defences between 1708 and 1714. Like the kitchen range, the chambers below the artillery platform had to be infilled to provide a firm base for the guns, but this packing has also since been removed, and it is now possible to visit the two surviving lower floors of the tower.

Theodore Dury's plan of the Castle in the early 18th century.

The gun platform and views from the Elphinstone Tower.

The Grand Battery.

It is suggested that visitors should make a tour of the wall walks which run along the east and north sides of the main enclosure of the Castle. The first stretch of this walk is occupied by the Grand (or seven gun) battery, the construction of which in 1689 necessitated the infilling of the kitchens below. (The parapet was reconstructed in the operations of 1708.) From here there are excellent views of the surrounding countryside, including the medieval bridge at the crossing of the Forth which gave Stirling such strategic importance, and the Abbey Craig where William Wallace's forces were gathered before the Battle of Stirling Bridge in 1297 (and which is now crowned by the Wallace Monument). Also in the valley, within a loop of the River Forth, are the ruins of the

The western walls.                    The crags on the west side.

26

royal Abbey of Cambuskenneth, the tower of which is a notable landmark. Closer at hand is Gowan Hill: it was the near proximity of this high ground which suggested the need for the massive strengthening of the eastern side of the Castle by the construction of the Grand Battery (it is of interest to note that the Young Pretender placed some of his guns on this hill when he attacked the Castle in 1746).

Continuing along the wall-walk, and crossing the North Gate, visitors reach the wall which overlooks the Nether Bailey. For most of its length this wall is a 16th century rebuilding, following a report of 1583 that part of it had collapsed. Within the main enclosure at this point is a pleasantly sheltered area behind the Chapel Royal and King's Old Building, which has been variously named as the Captain's, Governor's and Douglas Garden. At its centre is the shaft of a 17th century sundial, and tucked into a corner is a small, and much altered powder magazine which probably dates from Dury's works of the early 18th century. From the stretch of wall-walk behind this magazine there are splendid views westwards towards the hills around Loch Lomond. The near-vertical faces of the Castle rock on this side afforded magnificent natural protection, and obviated the need for major strengthening of the defences such as took place in the later 17th and 18th centuries on the south and east sides of the Castle.

The Douglas Garden.

The powder magazine.

## 13. THE 'LADY'S HOLE' AND 'KING'S KNOT'

The Upper Square is again reached by way of a transe between the King's Old Building and the Chapel Royal, and by re-entering the Palace and immediately leaving it through a door to the right the next point on the itinerary is reached. This small irregular enclosure was known from at least as early as the first years of the 18th century as the "Lady's Hole", perhaps because it was a favoured sitting-out area which commanded enjoyable views of the hills to the west of the castle. It also over-looked the enclosed Park and formal Gardens below. Traces of the so-called "King's Knot" and an adjoining parterre, which perhaps date from 1628, still provide clues to the lay-out of what must have been a very fine formal garden. Before the collapse of part of the west wing of the Palace at some date in the 17th century the "Lady's Hole" would have been rather smaller than now, but it is tempting to speculate that it may have opened into the Palace through loggias (arcaded galleries) such as were to be found in contemporary French palaces.

The King's Knot and parterre of the royal gardens.

A view across the
Counterguard.

The 'Lion's Den' at the
heart of the Palace.

The Counterguard and
*Bottom right* wall of the
Forework.

The suggested tour continues through a vaulted transe which runs beneath the south quarter of the Palace. Irregularities of the walls to either side of this transe are in part a result of the retention of earlier structures, which may be contemporary with the adjacent Forework built in about 1500. From this transe it is possible to make a detour into the central courtyard of the Palace, the "Lion's Den"; the origin of this name is uncertain, but it is at least an attractive possibility that James V allowed a lion which he had been given in 1537 to be exercised here. On the western side of the court traces of earlier doors and windows may be seen in the wall of the gallery which connected the two royal apartments; there used to be a stair from this gallery into the courtyard. Returning to the transe, and passing along it to its exit into the Lower Square, a modern door opening through the Forework wall on the right will be found. This door leads onto the stump of the western of the two semi-circular towers which used to flank the gate. It is possible that this may have been the College Tower, to which a reference was made in 1687.

From this stump the visitor overlooks the part of the Counterguard which served as a bowling green from at least the last decades of the 17th century. Traces of formal gardens may be observed in the terrace which runs along the southern side of the green. At the western end of this terrace, against the Prince's Tower, is a fragment of an earlier outer wall of the Counterguard, and at its base is the end of the balustraded parapet of the terrace, which was erected in 1628.

Visitors should follow the path along the side of the ramp leading from the Forework Gate, and pass the arched ends of the vaulted barrack chambers under the Queen Anne Battery of 1708-14. Beyond the range of barracks is a section of wall pierced by three arched casemates for guns. These were provided to allow defenders to fire along the external face of the Outer Defences in the area where the rock face becomes less steep, and therefore more vulnerable to attack. At the far end of the casemated wall is a stair leading to the covered way along the wallhead. The massive thickness of the early 18th century defences can be best appreciated on the higher level of the Queen Anne Battery, which overlooks the Guardroom Square. The defending soldiers on the wallhead were protected by a parapet, in front of which is a gently sloping earthen bank, known as a *glacis,* designed to absorb shot whilst allowing an unrestricted field of fire. At the outer corner of the Queen Anne Battery a passage leads to a projecting stone sentry box.

The vaulted barrack chambers.

## 16. THE FRENCH SPUR

The recommended route for visitors continues from the Queen Anne Battery down the ramp towards the Forework Gate, and back down the ramp leading to the Inner Gate; from here it follows the path past the vaulted barrack chambers of the Overport Battery to the French Spur. As first built, probably in 1559, the French Spur was a V-shaped projection with the base of the V towards the east, and with a rectangular indentation on its southern side to provide a protected position for firing along the ditch in front of the Castle walls. When it was remodelled in 1708, to perform a modified role in the new Outer Defences, a thick wall was built across the opening of the indentation with two casemates for guns at the enclosed lower level. By this means provision was made for two tiers of guns firing along the lengthened ditch, and there were further gun embrasures at the upper level only, which were directed to the north-east and south-east of the Castle. It may be noted that within the area of the French Spur there is also a second well, with its head adjacent to the casemates at the lower level.

From here visitors may leave the Castle by returning through the Inner Gate of the Outer Defences.

Views across the French Spur.

Printed in Scotland for HMSO by
CC 30554, Dd 287675 / HF 4176 C400 2/90.